It's My Wish That You Know

Written by **PHILIP A. EDLES**

Illustrated by Margaret Clayton

Order this book online at www.trafford.com
or email orders@trafford.com

Most Trafford titles are also available at major online book retailers.

 www.trafford.com

North America & international
toll-free: 844 688 6899 (USA & Canada)
fax: 812 355 4082

Our mission is to efficiently provide the world's finest, most comprehensive book publishing service, enabling every author to experience success. To find out how to publish your book, your way, and have it available worldwide, visit us online at www.trafford.com

ISBN: 978-1-6987-0437-1 (sc)
ISBN: 978-1-6987-0438-8 (e)

Trafford rev. 11/17/2020

Dedications

You have ten little fingers and ten little toes.
Two ears to hear and a beautiful nose.

Use them to feel, to listen, to grow,
you are capable and powerful,
it's my wish that you know.

You have a huge brain and a plenty large mouth, to wonder and figure, to speak and shout out.

Use them to question, to stand up,
to show, you are ready and able,
it's my wish that you know.

Not everyone knows this. It's my wish you go out. Tell them on the playground, in the street, all about.

"I have a plenty big mouth, a
big brain and much more,
you have these too, use them galore".

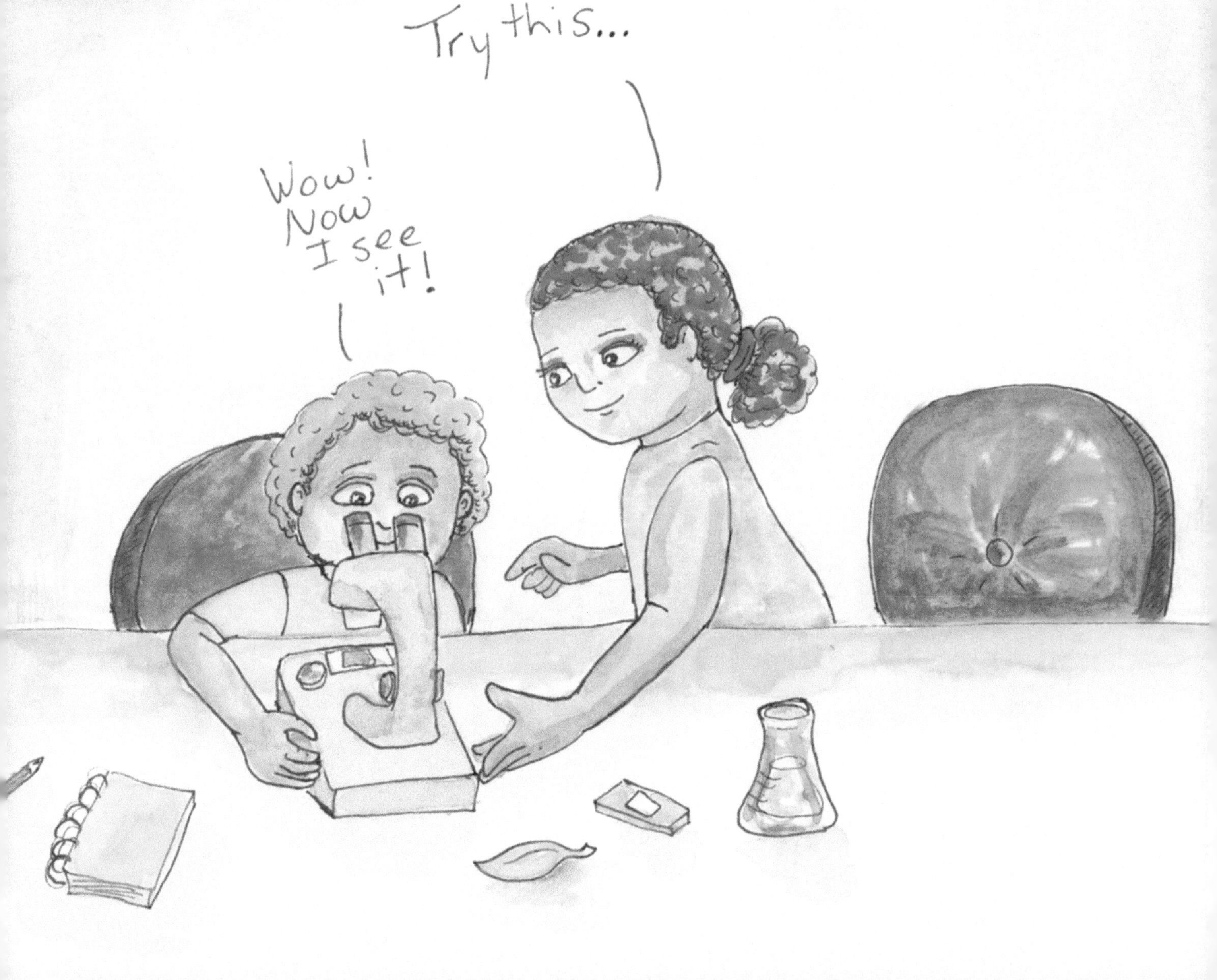
Try this...
Wow! Now I see it!

And you don't need a large mouth,
all your fingers or toes,
give a wink or a grunt, so everyone knows.

That your power comes from you being you,
without stepping on others, it's not easy to do.

But if my wish should come true
you will be brave and be strong,
you'll know when to stand up,
and fight...to get along.

You'll learn to absorb, not block
nor swallow whole.
It will make you mighty inside;
it's my wish that you know.

Printed in the United States
By Bookmasters